Forecasting Disasters

FLOODS

Trudy Becker

WWW.APEXEDITIONS.COM

Copyright © 2026 by Apex Editions, Mendota Heights, MN 55120. All rights reserved. No part of this book may be reproduced or utilized in any form or by any means without written permission from the publisher.

Apex is distributed by North Star Editions:
sales@northstareditions.com | 888-417-0195

Produced for Apex by Red Line Editorial.

Photographs ©: Shutterstock Images, cover, 1, 4–5, 14–15, 16–17, 20–21, 22–23, 26–27, 29, 30–31, 32–33, 34–35, 36–37, 42–43, 44–45, 50–51, 54–55, 56–57; iStockphoto, 6–7, 8–9, 10–11, 12–13, 58; Fareed Khan/AP Images, 18–19; Imagno/Brandstaetter Images/Hulton Archive/Getty Images, 24–25; Ezra Acayan/NurPhoto/Corbis News/Getty Images, 38–39; FeatureChina/Newscom, 41; Jose Robles/Aton Chile/AP Images, 46–47; Joe Raedle/Getty Images News/Getty Images, 48–49; Mario Tama/Getty Images News/Getty Images, 52–53

Library of Congress Control Number: 2025930334

ISBN
979-8-89250-660-1 (hardcover)
979-8-89250-695-3 (ebook pdf)
979-8-89250-678-6 (hosted ebook)

Printed in the United States of America
Mankato, MN
082025

NOTE TO PARENTS AND EDUCATORS

Apex books are designed to build literacy skills in striving readers. Exciting, high-interest content attracts and holds readers' attention. The text is carefully leveled to allow students to achieve success quickly.

TABLE OF CONTENTS

Chapter1
RISING WATER 4

Chapter 2
ALL ABOUT FLOODS 10

Chapter 3
EARLY FLOOD FORECASTING 20

That's Wild!
DAM DEATHS 28

Chapter 4
MODERN METHODS 31

That's Wild!
HOSPITAL ESCAPE 40

Chapter 5
FLOOD MODELS 42

Chapter 6
FUTURE FLOOD TOOLS 50

TIMELINE • 59
COMPREHENSION QUESTIONS • 60
GLOSSARY • 62
TO LEARN MORE • 63
ABOUT THE AUTHOR • 63
INDEX • 64

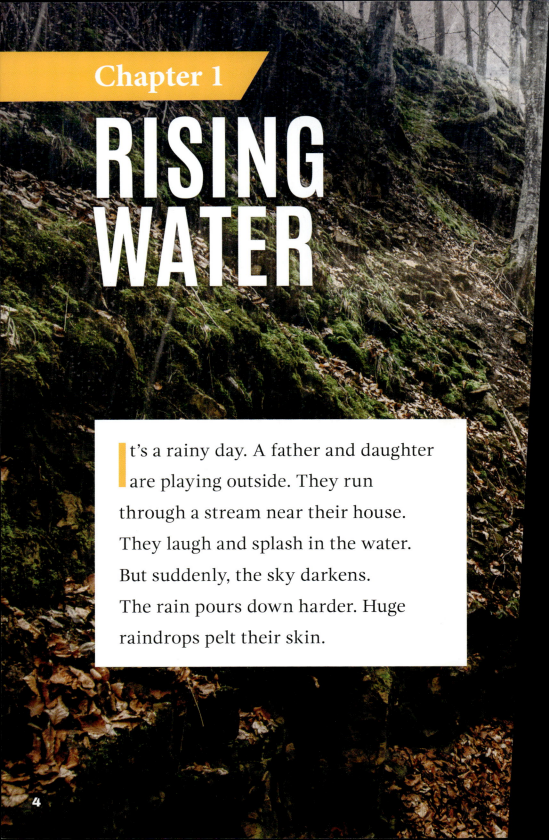

Chapter 1
RISING WATER

It's a rainy day. A father and daughter are playing outside. They run through a stream near their house. They laugh and splash in the water. But suddenly, the sky darkens. The rain pours down harder. Huge raindrops pelt their skin.

Floods are most likely to happen in summer and fall.

The dad looks up toward the house. He sees water running down the hill. Just then, a sound blares from his pocket. The dad pulls out his phone. The screen shows a weather alert. Their area has a flash flood warning.

Smartphone alerts can help people stay safe during floods.

It's important to stay off the roads during a flood.

The dad acts fast. He calls to his daughter. Together, they hurry back up the slippery hill. Then they run inside the house. From the window, they watch the stream. The water rushes and rushes. Then it rises. It flows over the banks. Soon, the water starts to sweep over the roads.

FLOOD SAFETY
Flood alerts often include safety tips. They tell people to move to high ground. People should also avoid areas near moving water. And they should never drive. Driving in floods has led to many deaths.

Chapter 2
ALL ABOUT FLOODS

Flooding is the most common type of natural disaster. A flood happens when an area has more water than it can handle. The water rushes over solid land. In some cases, it starts to fill up low areas. The water gets deeper and deeper.

Some floods happen after hurricanes.

Dry soil can soak up extra water, but wet soil floods quickly.

Flash floods are one type of flood. Storms often cause them. Flash floods can happen in just minutes. River floods are another type. In river floods, rivers or creeks gain water over time. Then the water overflows onto land. River floods can happen seasonally or during storms. Coastal floods are a third type. Water from the ocean goes onto shore.

Floods happen all over the world. They often take place near bodies of water. Mountains with streams are prone to floods. So are some lower areas, such as valleys.

Cities flood, too. Much of the ground is covered in concrete. The ground can't soak up the extra water. That causes extra runoff.

FUTURE FLOODS
Climate change affects flood conditions. Hotter temperatures melt glaciers faster. Heat also makes the air moister. That causes more rainfall. Climate change leads to more extreme storms, too. All these factors may bring more floods in the future.

In some countries, most of the land is a flood zone. Bangladesh is one example.

Some floods cause landslides, which can lead to major damage.

Floods cause terrible destruction. They ruin buildings. They sweep trees away. Water also makes structures moldy or unstable. That damage is expensive. For example, in 1993, extreme flooding hit the midwestern United States. The damage topped $30 billion.

MUD ANGELS

Arno, Italy, flooded in 1966. In just 24 hours, the city got 25 percent of its yearly rainfall. The water flooded art museums and libraries. It damaged valuable objects. Volunteers known as "mud angels" helped. They dug through the mud. They saved priceless items.

Floods kill more people than any other weather disaster. Most flood deaths come from drowning. Other times, sharp or heavy objects get swept up in the water. Then they crash into people. Floods lead to disease, too. Dirty water spreads deadly diseases such as cholera and typhoid.

2022 PAKISTAN FLOODS

In 2022, severe flooding hit Pakistan. Strong monsoons brought huge amounts of rain. Glacier melt added more water. Soon, one-third of the country was underwater. More than 1,700 people died from drowning and disease.

More than two million Pakistanis lost their homes in the 2022 floods.

Chapter 3

EARLY FLOOD FORECASTING

Floods were hard to forecast in the past. Instead of predicting floods, people tried to prevent future damage. For example, ancient people built flood walls. They also dredged rivers. They created draining systems, too.

Cloaca Maxima is part of an ancient Roman draining system.

However, people in the past did have some tools for prediction. Ancient Egyptians used tools called nilometers. The tools were tall structures. People put them in the Nile River. They measured how high the water rose. Then people compared water levels between years. Higher levels usually meant more flooding.

HELPFUL FLOODS

In ancient times, the Nile flooded every year. Its annual flooding could be disastrous. But some amount of flooding was necessary. The yearly flooding made the soil rich. That helped people grow crops.

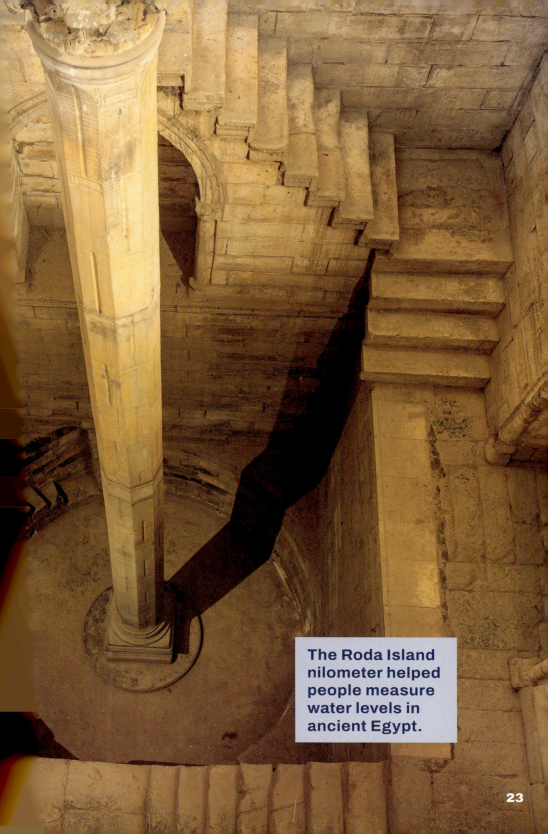

The Roda Island nilometer helped people measure water levels in ancient Egypt.

A drawing from the 1800s shows flooding in Europe.

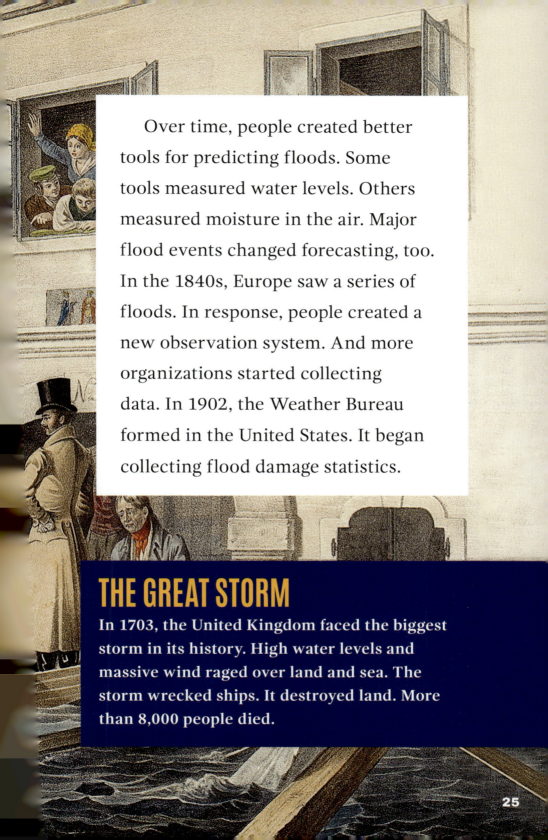

Over time, people created better tools for predicting floods. Some tools measured water levels. Others measured moisture in the air. Major flood events changed forecasting, too. In the 1840s, Europe saw a series of floods. In response, people created a new observation system. And more organizations started collecting data. In 1902, the Weather Bureau formed in the United States. It began collecting flood damage statistics.

THE GREAT STORM

In 1703, the United Kingdom faced the biggest storm in its history. High water levels and massive wind raged over land and sea. The storm wrecked ships. It destroyed land. More than 8,000 people died.

The new tools and data collection helped with forecasting. But the data was often incomplete. It was hard to predict floods more than a day ahead. Communicating flood information was hard, too. Information traveled slowly.

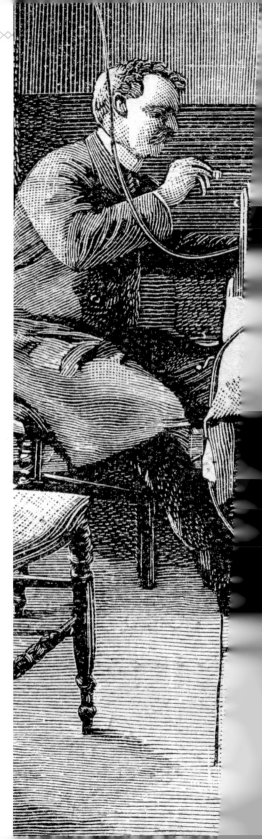

The invention of the telegraph in the 1800s helped forecasts spread faster.

That's Wild!

DAM DEATHS

Natural disasters often bring floods. But human actions can cause floods, too. In the 1840s, people built a dam. It was near Johnstown, Pennsylvania. The dam faced problems over the years. It failed more than once. So, builders fixed some pieces. But they left other parts unfixed.

In 1889, the area got a huge amount of rain. The weak dam failed again. It burst. The dam released a massive wall of water. The flood killed 2,200 people within minutes.

When the dam in Johnstown burst, the wall of water was more than 30 feet (9 m) tall.

Scientists use powerful computers to predict floods and other disasters.

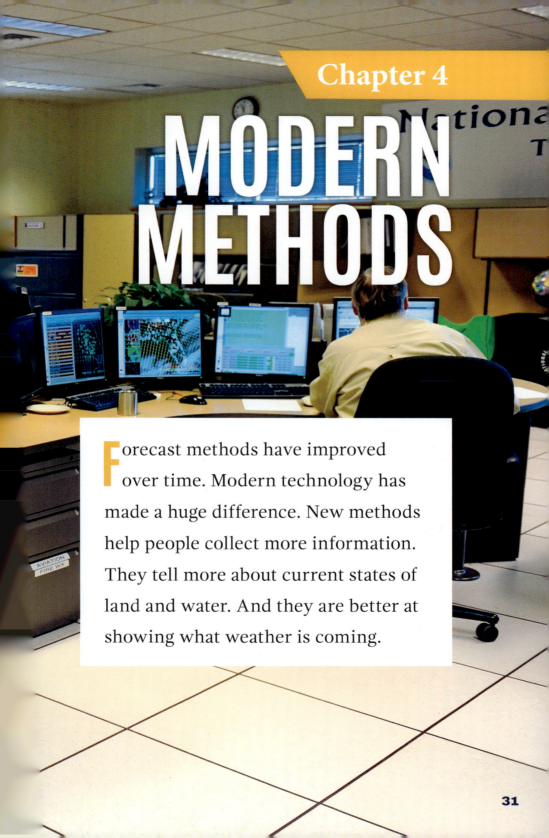

Chapter 4
MODERN METHODS

Forecast methods have improved over time. Modern technology has made a huge difference. New methods help people collect more information. They tell more about current states of land and water. And they are better at showing what weather is coming.

Radar is a major tool for predicting floods. Radar sends out radio waves. The waves hit something and bounce back. People can analyze the results. Radar is key for tracking precipitation. Precipitation is a main factor in most floods. Radar shows where intense rainfall will happen. Radar can also show how long rainfall will last.

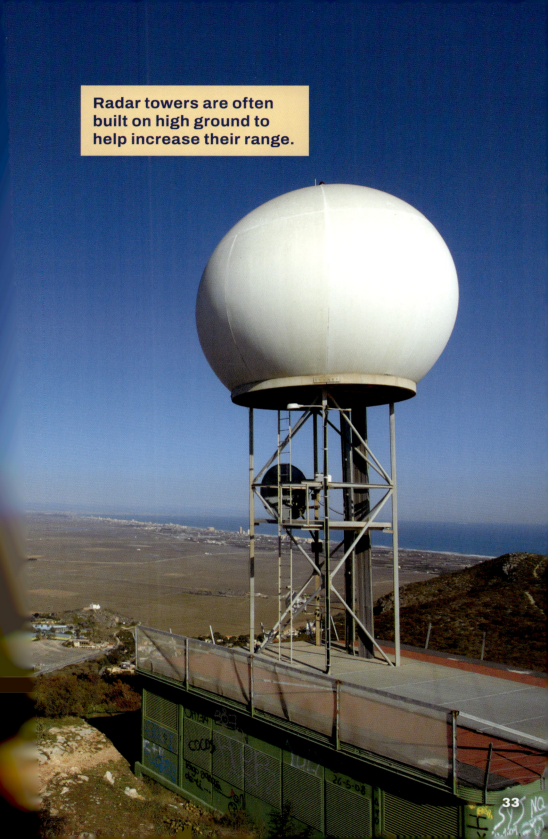
Radar towers are often built on high ground to help increase their range.

Satellites are another tool. Satellites are machines in orbit. They take images of Earth. The images are linked together to show how weather is moving. Scientists can spot cloud patterns that indicate storms. That gives hints about possible flooding.

Scientists use satellites to track hurricanes and other large storms.

USEFUL AREAS

Compared to radar, satellites don't give much detail about rain. However, satellites offer data from more places. For example, satellites can study oceans. Scientists get information about storms over the sea. Then they predict how the storms will move.

Stream gauges are other key tools. Stream gauges go directly into bodies of water. They track the water level. Modern gauges send their data digitally. Meteorologists analyze the water data. If flooding is likely, they can warn people days ahead of time.

In 2024, Tropical Storm Trami hit the Philippines. It was a devastating storm. But a variety of tools helped forecasters. Radar and satellites showed the storm was coming. Forecasters had some warning. So, many people were able to leave the area. They made it to safety.

TOOL TROUBLE

High-tech instruments can be hard to maintain. Stream gauges can break. Others get lost over time. That happened in several African nations. Some areas have fewer tools than before. Other places still don't have any flood tools.

During Tropical Storm Trami, two months' worth of rain fell in 24 hours.

That's Wild!

HOSPITAL ESCAPE

In 2021, enormous rainfall soaked Zhengzhou, China. Officials at a major hospital learned about the storm ahead of time. They were worried. So, the staff met. They discussed possible evacuation. They created plans.

The next day, water leaked into the hospital. It started flooding. So, staff began the evacuation. They safely moved more than 11,000 people out of the hospital. Early flood forecasts were key to their success. The hospital staff had enough time to prepare.

Chinese officials evacuate patients during the 2021 Zhengzhou flood.

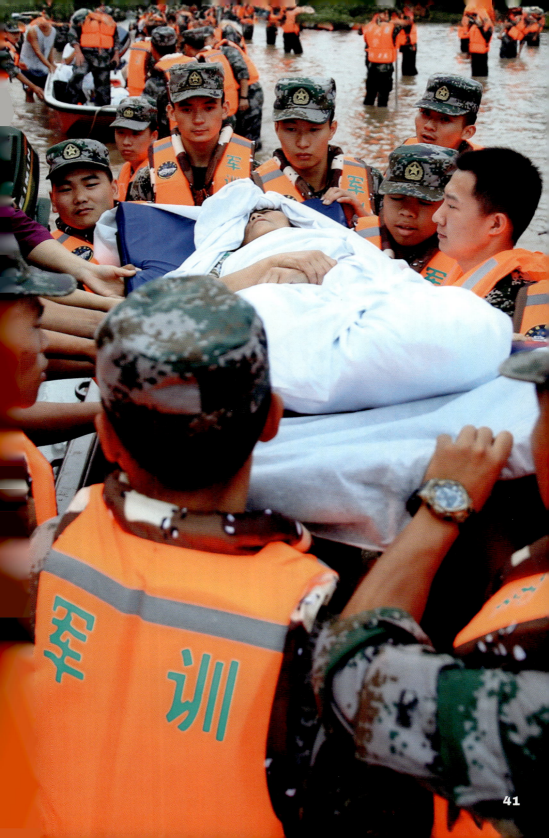

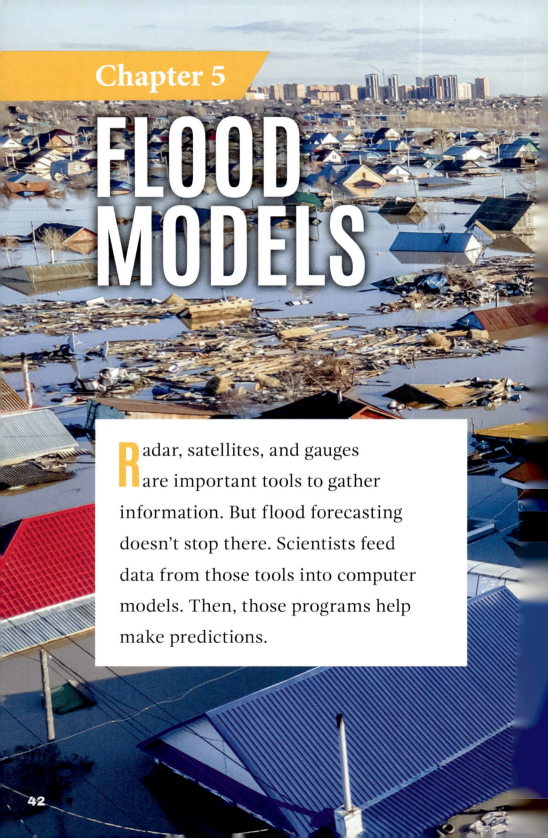

Chapter 5

FLOOD MODELS

Radar, satellites, and gauges are important tools to gather information. But flood forecasting doesn't stop there. Scientists feed data from those tools into computer models. Then, those programs help make predictions.

Better forecasting can help people escape before floods arrive.

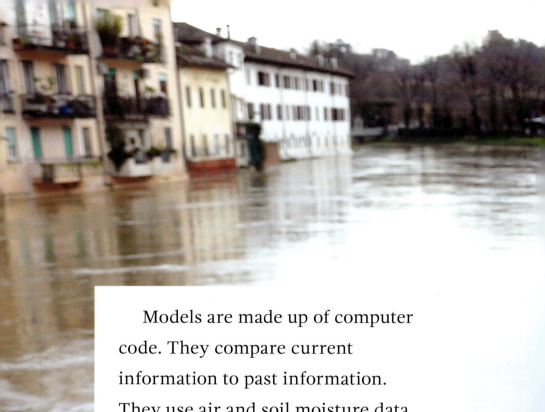

Models are made up of computer code. They compare current information to past information. They use air and soil moisture data. Precipitation and water levels are key pieces, too. Then the models make conclusions. Some can say how much rain usually leads to strong flooding in an area.

Scientists use tools called hydrometric probes to help monitor water levels.

45

Models often make a big difference. In 2023, scientists in Chile used a model called Flood Hub. It gave people a two-day warning about a flood. Many could evacuate in time. Models such as Flood Hub change over time. They get more information. They use it to improve their codes.

FILLING GAPS

Flood models can also fill in gaps. For example, some places don't have enough tools to collect data. But similar areas of land do supply information. So, models apply data from those areas. They use that information for predictions.

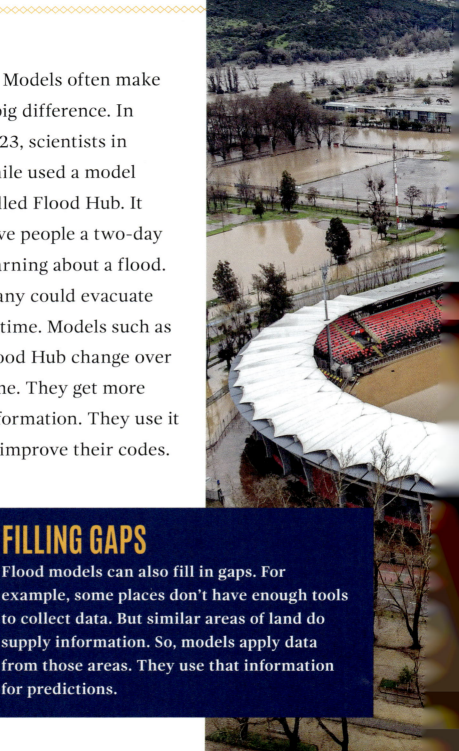

Water fills a stadium during a 2023 flood in Chile.

The flooding from Hurricane Milton damaged many homes and businesses.

Computer models supply lots of information. But humans still have to make forecast decisions. And communicating those decisions saves lives. That was the case in Florida in 2024. Hurricane Milton approached several major cities. Forecasters looked at all the data. They issued strong warnings. Wind and floods ravaged the area. But the warnings helped. Many people had left.

BAD COMMUNICATION

Sometimes, people don't receive strong warnings. For example, some areas of Europe flooded in 2021. Scientists warned officials ahead of time. But officials did not do enough to spread the word. Hundreds of people died.

Chapter 6

FUTURE FLOOD TOOLS

People continue to improve flood prediction tools. For example, scientists are developing new types of radar. They're creating better satellites, too. These advances help improve forecast speeds. People can predict floods quicker than ever before.

Alarm systems can warn people when floods are likely.

Drones are another modern tool. Drones can give detailed information on flooded areas. They can reach dangerous areas, too. Thermal cameras are another development. These tools measure heat. Using temperature differences, they spot the flow of water over land. Then scientists can learn which areas may flood.

SUPER-TOOLS

Some new forecasting tools can be used together. That makes them even more effective. For example, people put thermal cameras on drones. That way, forecasters get more information.

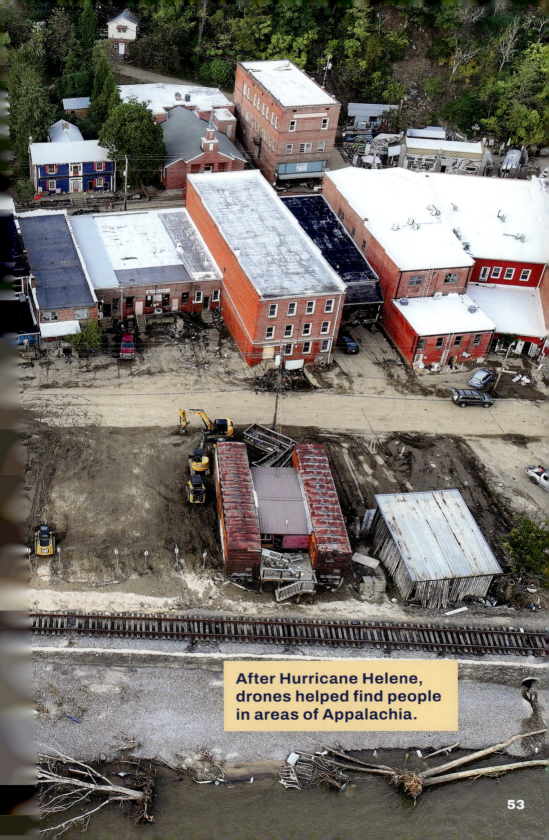

After Hurricane Helene, drones helped find people in areas of Appalachia.

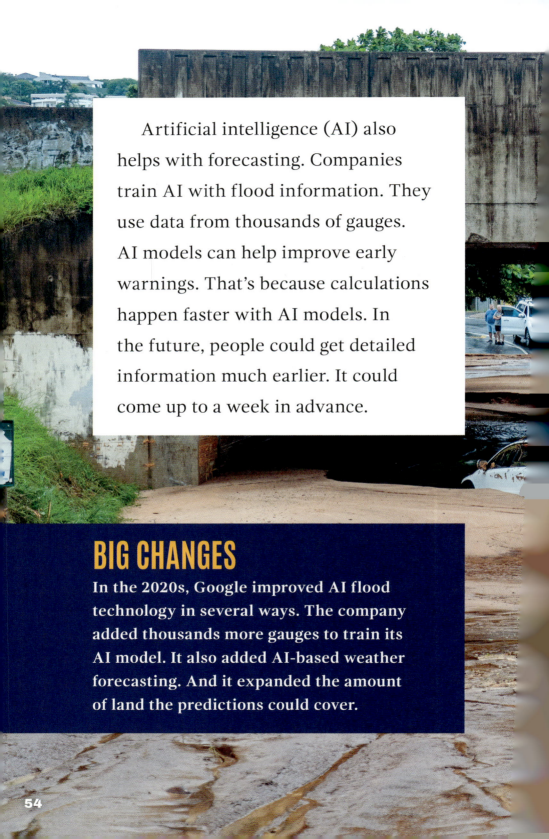

Artificial intelligence (AI) also helps with forecasting. Companies train AI with flood information. They use data from thousands of gauges. AI models can help improve early warnings. That's because calculations happen faster with AI models. In the future, people could get detailed information much earlier. It could come up to a week in advance.

BIG CHANGES

In the 2020s, Google improved AI flood technology in several ways. The company added thousands more gauges to train its AI model. It also added AI-based weather forecasting. And it expanded the amount of land the predictions could cover.

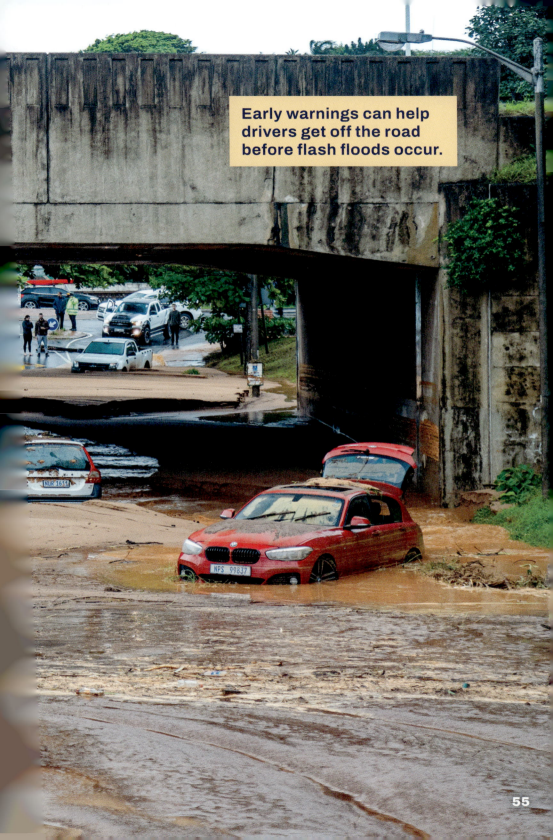

Early warnings can help drivers get off the road before flash floods occur.

People are creating better flood alert systems across the world. Many systems use smartphones. In the United States, Wireless Emergency Alerts do that. These messages include flash flood alerts. The messages contact millions of people. And they reach people quickly. Along with other technologies, better alerts can save more lives.

In the United States, more than 4,000 flood alerts are issued every year.

TIMELINE

1889 Rainfall causes a dam to burst in Johnstown, Pennsylvania, killing thousands.

1902 The Weather Bureau in the United States begins collecting flood damage statistics.

1993 Damage from flooding in the midwestern United States costs $30 billion.

2021 Poor communication leads to greater flood destruction in Europe.

2021 Hospital officials evacuate patients from a flooded hospital in Zhengzhou, China.

2022 A series of floods in Pakistan causes devastation.

2023 The Flood Hub model gives early information before flooding in Chile.

2024 Hurricane Milton floods parts of Florida.

2024 Tropical Storm Trami hits the Philippines.

COMPREHENSION QUESTIONS

Write your answers on a separate piece of paper.

1. Write a paragraph that describes the main ideas of Chapter 3.

2. What do you think is the most important tool for predicting floods? Why?

3. When did the Johnstown dam fail?
   A. 1889
   B. 1902
   C. 2024

4. How could data from similar areas of land help predict floods in places without flood data?
   A. Similar areas of land might have similar flood conditions.
   B. Scientists would get more money to invent better tools.
   C. Predictions cannot use data from similar areas of land.

5. What does **meteorologists** mean in this book?

Meteorologists analyze the water data. If flooding is likely, they can warn people days ahead of time.

    A. people who study weather

    B. people who cause floods

    C. people who stop floods

6. What does **effective** mean in this book?

*That makes them even more **effective**. For example, people put thermal cameras on drones. That way, forecasters get more information.*

    A. dangerous

    B. useful

    C. breakable

Answer key on page 64.

GLOSSARY

artificial intelligence
Computer systems that can learn and change without following new instructions.

climate change
A dangerous long-term change in Earth's temperature and weather patterns.

dredged
Scooped out material from the bottom of rivers.

drones
Aircraft that people control from far away or that work on their own.

flash flood
A sudden rush of water caused by heavy rain.

gauges
Tools that measure the water levels of rivers or streams.

monsoons
Strong winds that cause seasons of very wet or dry weather in an area.

orbit
A curved path around an object in space.

precipitation
Water that falls to the ground as rain, sleet, hail, or snow.

runoff
Extra water the land can't take in. This water flows along the ground into lakes, rivers, and streams.

TO LEARN MORE

BOOKS

Adamson, Thomas K. *Hurricane Katrina*. Bellwether Media, 2022.

Becker, Trudy. *2022 Pakistan Floods*. Apex Editions, 2024.

Bell, Samantha S. *Engineering for Floods*. Focus Readers, 2021.

ONLINE RESOURCES

Visit **www.apexeditions.com** to find links and resources related to this title.

ABOUT THE AUTHOR

Trudy Becker lives in Minneapolis, Minnesota. She likes exploring new places and loves anything involving books.

INDEX

alerts, 6, 9, 56
artificial intelligence, 54

climate change, 14
coastal floods, 13
communication, 26, 49
computer models, 42, 44, 46, 49, 54

damage, 17, 20, 25
data collection, 25–26, 35, 37, 42, 44, 46, 49, 54
deaths, 9, 18, 25, 28, 49
disease, 18
draining systems, 20
drones, 52

evacuations, 38, 40, 46

flash floods, 6, 13, 56
Flood Hub, 46
flood walls, 20

gauges, 37–38, 42, 54

Hurricane Milton, 49

Johnstown flood, 28

meteorologists, 37
mud angels, 17

nilometers, 22

Pakistan floods of 2022, 18
precipitation, 32, 44

radar, 32, 35, 38, 42, 50
river floods, 13, 22

satellites, 34–35, 38, 42, 50

thermal cameras, 52
Tropical Storm Trami, 38

Weather Bureau, 25

ANSWER KEY:

1. Answers will vary; 2. Answers will vary; 3. A; 4. A; 5. A; 6. B